The Conscience *of* My Other Being

The Conscience *of* My Other Being

by William Walsh

Cherokee Publishing Company
Atlanta, Georgia
2005

Library of Congress Cataloging-in-Publication Data
Walsh, William

This book is printed on acid-free paper which conforms to the American National Standard Z39.48-1984 Permanence of Paper for Printed Library Materials. Paper that conforms to this standard's requirements for pH, alkaline reserve and freedom from groundwood is anticipated to last several hundred years without significant deterioration under normal library use and storage conditions.

Manufactured in the United States of America

First Edition

ISBN: 0-87797-313-X

12 11 10 09 08 07 06 05   10 9 8 7 6 5 4 3 2 1

 Cherokee Publishing Company is an operating division of the Larlin Corporation, P O Box 1730, Marietta, Georgia 30061

*For my
Mother and Father
and to
the memory of
Dr. I. Lamar Maffett
(1930-1999)*

Acknowledgments

Many of these poems have been published whole or in part in the following journals: *The Allegheny Review, The Charlotte Poetry Review, The Cotton Boll, Devil's Millhopper, Kestrel, Mississippi Valley Review, The New Laurel Review, The Pittsburgh Quarterly Review, Scroll, Slant,* and *The Timber Creek Review*. In addition, some poems have been previously published in a chapbook, *The Ordinary Life of a Sculptor*.

"The Death that Never Occurred" was published in *Crossroads: A Southern Culture Annual*, edited by Ted Olson and published by Mercer University Press (available in September 2005).

I would like to acknowledge Kathy Sims Collier, my seventh grade teacher, who many years ago opened up my world when she taught me to write poems and stories; Dr. I. Lamar Maffett, a wonderful professor and the first reader of my poems during my college years – a very funny man who gave me scores of encouragement as well as enjoyment in his English classes; David Bottoms and Jack Myers, poets and teachers; and, novelist John Williams for his friendship and thoughts regarding the early versions to many of these poems. Ken Boyd, thank you very much for publishing my poems. And, most especially, I would like to thank my wife, Elaine, for her wonderful support and ability to tolerate my crazy ideas. Also, to my beautiful children, Jon, Alex, and Olivia.

Table of Contents

I. Unsophisticated Time

II. A Darkness Touching My Skin

III. Double-Live Cowboy

IV. Thirty Minutes Before Sundown

Unsophisticated Time

*So the Earth endures, in every petty matter
And in the lives of men, irreversible.
And it seems a relief. To win? To lose?
What for, if the world will forget us anyway.*

– Czeslaw Milosz

*I changed with them inward, toward
The weedy heart of the junkyard,
For I knew that Doris Holbrook
Would escape from her father at noon.*

– James Dickey

In Anticipation of Spending Several Nights in Jail

I opened the window this morning after a hot shower
and the neighborhood air rushed in against my skin.

My neighbor, Jerry, scuttled to the edge of his grass
for the newspaper, puttered around his manicured lawn

as he sucked down a Bloody Mary, chomping the celery
like it's the only thing in the entire world left to eat

and someone on a hang glider might swoop down
like a giant ferocious owl and steal it. "Hey Jerry!" I yelled,

"I don't wear pajamas." I figured he doesn't wear pajamas,
just waltzes around the house like Hugh Hefner

puffing a stogie, calls his bookie to drop a grand
on the Cowboys. Jerry's an out-of-shape scratch golfer

on his third wife. He writes a daily sports column for the *Post Courier,*
invites me over for summer cocktails and cookouts

with his friends, who, like him, wear brown fedoras
and are married to blondes named Doll

or Bunny. He listens to Dizzy Gillespe records.
His shirt reads, "Babe-a-holic" and his friends laugh

a lot at him for his horny-jerk self. But on this morning
the sun screamed off the chrome of his '57 Corvette, a forty-seven

year-old red dream I want to joy ride, just like that girl
in high school, just one spin around the block, the dream girl

who was always so golden that no matter who you ended up loving,
she was the one all women are compared to, how you watched her

cheerleader moves, the air and sunlight dancing around her
like time and space were invented for her body. But you never

spoke to her because you were some brand of farm animal.
Maybe she was so golden that one single word spoken to her

would have imploded the known universe. How many years
has it been since you saw her? Wherever she is today,

she's still golden, still wrapped in blue jeans, sparkling
white sneakers, some guy's football jacket draped over her shoulders.

She isn't gone. She's always there, ringing in your ears, forever,
like the thickness of air when glass shatters into silence.

I've decided, tonight, I'm going to steal Jerry's Corvette,
roll it quietly down the street, pop the clutch

at the bottom of the hill and laugh with the engine's roar
for balance and my obsession with unity.

Maybe I mean nudity. Me and his car. Naked as I drive
searching for the golden girl. It takes awhile,

enough time must pass to extinguish the fear, to say what
you longed to say, tell everyone who knows a girl like

Becky Palmer in Southaven, Mississippi, "One day
a long time ago, one golden summer, I fell in love

with you." Shouldn't the world know and shouldn't Becky know, too,
if for no other reason than to explain the theft

of Jerry's Corvette and driving naked from Atlanta to Memphis,
and why so many years later I would be calling her from jail.

Tourettes

– for a former student with this affliction

Red terror
        as if I am being hacked with a machete,
never dying, just screams, a howling

dog everyone can hear two rooms away
        through the bathroom walls. I can't, can't shop
at the mall, go to the movies, school, or stop

the wild goose from breaking loose
        behind this levied miscarriage, busting, spinning,
an unbalanced gyroscope in my mind

whipping fragmented bursts of motion. My words, uncontrollable
        ticks that I can only guess are a past life
I've disrupted, an unhinged spirit breaking through

the black tunnel of nerve endings, the spitting sparks
        of a live wire crackling in the street. Echolalia,
repeating what was just said, the word

that was just said, what
        I just said – I am a woman,
a deep canyon with a U-turn. When my professor says

Roethke, I say *Roethke*. It's arduous
        to sit in the same room with me. Most people hate
working – day after day – I dream of working

in an office with people, typing
        steadily without punching all the keys at once, sitting
in a meeting around a large wooden table,

drinking coffee, Danish pastries, my opinion essential
      to the company's future.
Just for ten minutes. This would be heaven. Heaven.

Sometimes Lying is the Only Way Out of Trouble

Sometimes nothing feels so good as being drunk
and lying in the wet grass
at midnight. It's even better
if it's your lawn and not the neighbor's
or the grass in the park.

It's when you're in the wet grass
staring at the black star-dotted sky
that you actually believe you could fall
asleep right there. Sometimes,
you do. Other times you wake up
in jail next to some drunken stiff
and you look around at all the losers
and shake your head and wonder
where you are and how you got there
because something must be afoul
since you are respectable and well-known in some circles.

And then the morning comes, and most
of the other drunks are waking up
when the deputy takes roll call and you're ashamed
to answer when your name is called, but then you do
and sort of give thanks that no one has thrown up on you
or you on them or that you had to fight
some bum for a cot or space on the floor
and you hope you didn't do anything
really obscene or try to hit a cop.

Then the deputy says you can make one telephone call
but first you ask what city you're in, and

you realize that you have no friends
in town, so your next question is
about posting bail and a lawyer. One thousand dollars
later on the credit card you step outside the jail
and it's all concrete and black top
and not a blade of grass around. You hop a taxi
to the airport, a one-way coach ticket
back to your postage stamp of civility, and you leave
everything to the attorney. Then, standing in your front yard
you crank the mower and spend several hours
manicuring the lawn, making sure
each blade of grass is perfect
and when you're done, you're sweating
a really good ass-busting sweat, and you think that maybe
it was all a dream and you begin to feel
good about your life. Then your wife
walks outside with the portable telephone
and says it's for you, someone from the Myrtle Beach Police.

Espionage

Kirk, my private detective-friend,
has helped me on occasion run license plates
of women who've given me that look

we all look for. Information
makes us feel closer, powerful, anything about her
we don't already know – address, annual income,

marital status, does she own or rent,
education, all the information needed
to know if it's worth pursuing. Espionage

begins very young, innocently
in grade school, trying to find out
the pretty girl's name

sitting across the hall in another classroom.
We wrap ourselves in secret loves
like a thick cotton sweater, mysterious

because we can't explain
the attraction, yet, we're scared,
for even though she's at work,

somehow you know when you drive past her house,
she will be standing in the front yard
watering the chrysanthemums. But we drive by

regardless, because we know enough
that we could pretend it was coincidental,
a wrong turn. How funny. And then, how nice.

Burying My Dog

I brush past death with my ear flaps on.
Threads of sound follow. The untroubled neighbor kids

footfall into my dark tracks. The flash bouncing
on the ground guides them single file

through the woods to the spade-bent tree,
to the relaxed muslin-wrap that I carry

as once I carried love as gently from the shelter,
now to where lesser gardens grow under the slivered moon.

I hold a steady light and speak to each of them
in their own language over the small mound swell.

Want Ad

– for Jack Myers

I have this theory –
it's like buying a used car: reads well,
sounds good at first, but you can
bet your ass there's a reason
why it's on the market.

I'd like to place a personal ad
in the *Constitution* for a week, see
who writes back:

> *Short, crabby, balding 40ish guy, w/ an
> attitude problem, hates cats and kids, almost
> finished high school, unemployed, but
> looking, wants someone completely different
> than my other wives, prefers someone
> near bus routes. Definately a Democrat. I
> kiss on the first date, sometimes sooner if
> possible. Be honest – tell me about yourself
> – picture mandatory. I could change.*

You never want to oversell the merchandise. Sometimes
just driving down the road with the radio blaring out
"Long Cool Woman in a Black Dress" is all you need.
Makes me feel like crying.

Chilean Nights

My crazy love, see the llama
in August as tradition serves us
when we drink Coca-Cola
and look out over the horizon
on this somber plateau – rivers,
pathways, and thundering sky. Don't
let marriage be mapped into ritual. It is more
than a peccadillo. Be my love in the deep blue
billows when lightning crackles deep
and dark in the naked woods
of anger and sheets of rain pound
our bodies. Remember when we first rode
the llama and brushed the hair of the alpaca,
and they spoke to us and we had a conversation
in their native language called *duende*.

The Death that Never Occurred

Antom Sigular
Co F 45 Reg NY Inf Vol
8-28-29   2-23-86

The grave stone was mossy cool,
the abbreviated text chiseled deep by hand,

and as I ran my fingers along the grooves
of the letters, I could feel the lives of my ancestors

spiriting forward, generations later, the homestead still standing,
cut from the bone of sweat and the yellow fog

of dust swirling though Chautauqua County. We never met
but I am learning about your life

as my family traces your movements
through the Battle of the Wilderness

back to the safety of Union tents, open-fire
kettles and powered rifles

stacked like firewood. You lived
on beyond the war, and even late

in life, a daughter was born to this world
and though you died two years after, she lived a life

that led to me through her son's son. But now
I live in enemy territory, sleeping

with the Confederacy's daughter and her ancestor
crosscut by bullets at Chancellorsville

never knew his son still womb-tied, how he lived
a life and so on and so on and so on

until here she and I met in the modern world
under old battle flags. Outnumbered

at Chancellorsville, Stonewall Jackson's last
powerful thrust, the fearsome fighting

of the 11th corp of German immigrants
stood through thick underbrush and a deluge of fire

to free men they would never know,
and if the front line had broken

to scatter and fight hand to hand
with Johnny Reb or if the stones

and nails blasted from the cannons
found your flesh though the brush fires and blue smoke

of death, if one bullet had strayed on line,
or if you had made any decision

to move left or right at the wrong time among the timbers,
my history would have never been written.

Mowing the Yard of a Woman Whose Name I Have Forgotten

The summer I was fifteen
      I learned how to do everything
            left-handed. A new world rose

from the unbalanced: slow curve balls
      hung like apples, letters
            scribbled to friends proclaimed my new passion,

how the CIA would honor a man
      with ambidextrous talents. Against
            the mailbox with painted daisies, she stood

smiling, white blouse, tennis shoes
      fresh as a baseball, red stitching
            lipstick and small hoop earrings.

I mowed lawns that summer, muscular
      and textured like river water, form
            and continuity guiding

the Briggs & Stratton
      over the green laziness,
            a tender masculinity that could brush

back a young girl's hair
      as she closed her eyes to be kissed.
            She was left-handed, too, a brunette

whose husband sold life insurance
        across the country, out on Monday, home
                by Friday. Her house was immaculate.

She asked me to cut her lawn
        once a week. It could have been love,
                but it was more like a curious infatuation,

and I needed the money.
        In the circular weeks I came back
                more often to finish the jobs I had purposefully left

unfinished – trimming the hedges, sweeping
        the walkway, or washing her car.
                Each afternoon I stroked

the long metal catcher over the surface,
        swooshing bugs and grass over the fence
                into her neighbor's yard

while she read novels and watched me
        squeak around in my wet tennis shoes.
                Afterwards, when I jumped in to cool off,

she showed me how my hands
        in motion with her body
                brought about little deaths,

clenched fists, and warmth from shower water.
        She desired closeness,
                something

she had not known in some time.
        She wanted to be a dancer, a doctor, a singer.
                She grew up in the breeze

and freshness of the country,
        met her husband in Bakersfield
                at a dusty airport landing strip.

It bothers me that I have forgotten her
        name, an insensitivity equal to lying
                and moving away

without saying good-bye. When she
        was five, her younger sister died,
                and her mother, some days later,

found her sister's footprints in the dirt
        in the front yard and built (something)
                over them to keep the wind from blowing them away.

II

A Darkness Touching My Skin

You might come here Sunday on a whim.
Say your life broke down. The last good kiss
you had was years ago.

– Richard Hugo

Since my idiot childhood the world has been
Trying to tell me something. There is something
Hidden in the dark.

– Robert Penn Warren

The Letter Back Home

My world is not my world. I'm back
to the egg; exhausted
from my flight. Fourteen hours
from Montpelier and trying to beat the winter storm
headed my way, I boarded the wrong plane
twice then returned home to a $1300 checking error.

But worse, sadly, I returned
to learn of the death of a man
who was a great influence
on my life. I was out of town
and missed his funeral.
He was my professor, the first
man who brightened my eyes
to the wonders of Coleridge.

Tomorrow is my birthday.
I have nothing
special planned. Exercising
in my living room
where my sofa would be if I owned one.
My body feels sluggish. Three days home
now and the notches
are falling into place. Six months ago
Caroline kicked me out, two suit cases
jammed with wrinkled clothes. Divorce lingers
on the horizon so the girls
live with her. Yesterday, Caroline said
she never wanted to see me
again. I cannot believe
I was so bad.

Your words on this rainy afternoon
warm the house. I'm eating
instant soup, a cup
of coffee, watching Duke basketball.

My dog is praying to his God
that I drop my toast
on the floor. Your current peace of mind
fits you well. Your health, no doubt,
a result of climate. I am miserable. I'm disgusted
with my behavior because I am not a good friend.
I have been wrong about so much
in life. Can I start over
with you? Tonight, I'm drunk
in love over the art
we call children.

Quoting your letter, "I had
a wonderful dream about you
the other night. Made me feel
like we actually spent time together....
God damn you. I miss you, and you don't
write back." Please forgive my behavior
these past thirty years. I hand out heartache
like windshield flyers. Good things
do happen. I've been awarded
a fellowship to study
in Italy. Since being kicked out,
some dark clouds of my mystery
are lifting, but I cannot bear
to cook. Most evenings
I eat dinner at *Marie's*,
drink hazel nut coffee,
and pick up women since my sex
appeal to my estranged wife
is like putting on a wet bathing suit. Mostly,

I sit in the kitchen with Marcel
Dufour's daughter, Marianne,
writing a paper on the fusion
of painting and poetry. She asks
a mouthful of questions. Sometimes,
I make up stories to please her imagination.

Marcel lets me wait tables when the women are single.
There is no great energy within me, and I have been failing
to teach my students very well. Such energy
in their misunderstood childhoods
but I can not lift a finger to give a damn.

There is a darkness touching my skin
beneath my clothes.

I mourn my professor's death
because I never took the time – made
the effort – to know him
all these years, when
in fact, I could have.

Tuesday Morning in My Old Neighborhood

A mother and her two daughters
walked to the bus stop and waited

with the other children for the morning
sun to break through the thinning trees

of their hand-me-down lives.
They stood talking

about last night's trick
or treating, and some children still

had the ashes and dust of make-up
around their eyes, sleepy

from staying up late and counting
the bounty. They held their school books

and lunch boxes with *Jolly Ranchers* and *Mello Cups*
hidden underneath their bologna and peanut butter sandwiches

and *Oreo* cookies. There was just enough chill
in the air to know it was coming, the fall

weather and the hibernation of their bones, when
their house exploded, sending

a billion tooth picks whirling
through the air, breaking windows for six blocks.

A plume of smoke rose like a large tornado
targeting only one house. For days,

the street was filled with cars driving by to see what
a house looks like when it's been ripped apart

by a leaky gas line. The newspaper said
the twins almost stayed home from school

because they ate too many *Sweet Tarts*.
As the cars passed, they stopped

one by one at the hot chocolate stand
and made their donation, sipping the warmth.

She and her husband didn't have much
insurance. They rented an apartment

while the house was rebuilt, then moved
back in, and each morning

she and the girls walked to the bus stop. Then she
walked back home and opened the front door,

entering the new house, trusting
as she always was. And each time

she closed or opened a door, she could hear
the explosion and smell the smoke

the same way a soldier can feel
the itch of an amputated foot. At night,

she stretched out in bed, and listened to the house
creak and worried about many things.

The Blood Running Through Us

Our old bones keep us safe
in this world when life moves too fast

for evolution. I see it as my sons
and I walk through *Alligator Adventure*

in Myrtle Beach, the flattened lumps basking
in the sun, half petrified rock and half fallen tree stump

waiting for the brave or the stupid
and then coming alive with ferocity. It's hard to believe

a link fence can protect us. Fifteen years ago, my friend
killed himself after his little girl fell

from his shoulders. As quick
as it took to scream, she was gone

as they swarmed upon her. I helped his wife
clean his office, the small splatters

of blood on the dust jackets
of his favorite books. I pulled the carpet

completely off the floor and primed
and painted the walls a darker color.

I had no answer for the silence
thundering through the house, and then

one winter day she, too, was gone,
a new life some place

where the ancient world could not find her. I know
it was torture and despair driving him

through the forest of primal crying
and that he was unable to reconcile

his failures. But it goes deeper
than this, far into the well of our dark ancestry,

into a physiology of genomes
that I know nothing about. Life is

simply life, and gradually, we ease back
into who we have always been

and what we are most comfortable with, unaware
that change is temporary

as we search for what causes no pain.
There is inside each of us a scream

rushing to escape, and as I walk over the cat-walk
of floating logs, my grip is too strong on their small hands

and my boys try to pull away, so I hold on
even tighter, because the gators

with their eyes closed are lazy
until there's reason to move,

and therefore, like them, we are
destined to be who we are

yet so much more with our blood
flowing through a deeper river.

Visiting the VA Hospital

Grandfather, they didn't call you by your name,
a terrible trick for a man struggling
to remember anything. The staff didn't know you
sank in the ship's kitchen, though they figured
you had served. An apology to time,
you and the other soldiers with no money
and nowhere to go, a concentration camp
(of minimal comfort), a place to watch the past
die with some respect, finally saying we are sorry
that we killed, we are sorry we peeled potatoes for the troops.

It's been years since we played golf
together. You were fading then as I watched
you walk the fairway as though you could have walked off
the edge of the earth and not have known the difference.
Having never parred a hole in my life, I won the first three holes.

Rained out in the clubhouse, I thought how lonely
you looked staring out the window for a break
in the clouds as though the game
was the only thing you could rely upon.

In the hospital room you bolted from the green plastic chair
to punch and jab the invisible opponent, dark
pee stains circling your pant leg. You darted
across the room to swipe your roommate's baseball cap
and instinctively placed it on your great-grandson.
I had to believe this was a prophecy. I had to believe
in what you said when you touched me
on the chest with your small soft hand
as though passing on to me what I should always remember,
I lost something.

Leading you away to change your pants,
they told us not to say good-bye. You
would cry, and within two minutes
forget we had visited.

The VA hospital staff knew nothing
about you, or the time when I was eleven:
my brothers and I were watching *Jeopardy*
and you were the answer –
golfer, boxer, baseball man.

Bless You

This isn't pretty. I will warn you now. It was my downfall
saying "Bless you" to the young blonde
standing in line at Trust Company Bank. She sneezed
as I waited to cash a check as quickly as possible
from a guy I suspected as not having any money. I'd like
                    to tell you he was Mexican
but that would be politically incorrect
and you'd think I was a bigot, which I'm not,
but I do like details, plenty of details,
and his being Mexican has nothing to do with why
I was cashing the check so quickly.
He just seemed unscrupulous. From here on out
whenever something is politically correct
I'll type "p. c." If it's not
politically correct, "n.p.c."
This will save any potential typesetter valuable time
when I hit pay dirt and this poem becomes anthologized
or perhaps, just published somewhere, and in the long run,
in the big scheme of this swirling orb
of beauty we call earth, with a little disaster thrown in
for balance, my abbreviations
"p.c." and "n.p.c." will save ink and pulp. (p.c)
And, yes, you, the reader, listen up
to this... I'm directing this to you,
lughead – anything I can do
to save the planet (p.c.) I will.
I want to save this earth (p.c.)
and I suggest you do the same. (p.c.)

Saying "Bless you" was politically correct.
I omitted "God" intentionally, of course,
wanting to be non-denominational

in my conjecture (p.c.) and yes, she was young
and pretty and fairly innocent-looking. (n.p.c.)
She wasn't wearing a wedding band; however,
I never intended this as a come-on. I mean it.
Yes, normally I might have flirted
with her (p.c./n.p.c.?), but in truth,
I'm married, and I mean this, too, I just wanted to
cash this check, take my money
to Kroger, buy groceries to feed my kids,
and get my wife off my back
for the crummy job I have, then
meet an old high school friend at Café Intermezzo
to see how he's been since paroled
for stealing a cop car. (n.p.c./p.c.) Okay, I apologize
            for that remark
about my wife gnawing at my nerves, but she does
sometimes, and yes, I know,
I get on her nerves, too,
but that doesn't make my remarks right. Life isn't a contest
to see who wins the Irritation Competition
in the Olympic Marital Games. It's just, well, that's
how my day was going. Down hill. All I said
to this young sexy thing was "Bless you." (n.p.c.)
        Is that a crime? Or am I just a schmoozer, a schmuck,
a schnook? Am I just a guy stranded in the old way
of doing things? I didn't even smile at her.
I don't smile. I smirk,
just raise my lip a little
upward slightly and brighten my eyes. I didn't wink.
I'm not the winking type. If I wink
I end up looking like a cat with sand in his eye
whose next move is to paw at it
until he's crying. Why
did I say cat and not dog? Should I
give dogs equal time?
They have plenty of time in my other poems,

but if having a dog in this poem will calm
your sensitivities (p.c.) I'll accommodate.
           My dog's name is ROGER, a fox terrier.
Sorry. I never thought
about the choice I made – a male dog instead of a female.
I won't say a bitch. (n.p.c.) I don't like the connotation
behind the word. And why
a fox terrier? Do I have something against German Shepherds
or English Sheepdogs? No! Of course not. (P.C.)
I love dogs (p.c.) and I kind of like cats (pseudo-p.c.).
I love kids (very p.c.) – maybe
I'll run for governor with that on my ticket.

VOTE FOR ME. I LOVE CHILDREN.

Will that get me elected? If not, what will?
I'll have my picture taken (P.C.)
with a whole slew of kids, boys and girls: a Black, an Oriental,
a WASP, a Chicano, a Russian (to calm the peace-niks), a paraplegic in a
wheel chair,
a Jew, a child with Downe's syndrome,
a child feminist, kids whose mothers are members of NOW,
and children whose father were straight
but are now gay, some who were straight, switched to gay,
but switched back to straight
and now can't decide. I'll have a Southern Baptist
and whatever religions I can find, even
those two brothers kicked out
of the Boy Scouts because they're atheists, and an AIDS
infected child. I'll have an all girls
little league team and boys
who tap dance – all of us
sitting in front of a glowing fireplace
with an Irish Setter, (all of this very, very P.C.) just one
big happy family, no hate or prejudice, just love
of mankind. I'll change my politics (p.c.)

to suit your agenda, you the voting masses,
the ticket punchers, the beautiful moms
with two kids in an SUV waltzing
down the highway in the slow lane at fifty-five.

I apologize, that's a description of *Leave It To Beaver*,
a false representation of life in America.

Are my true colors showing though? I feel terrible.
I feel like I keep slipping up with you.
I'm really a nice guy once you get to know me.

    VOTE FOR ME. YOU'LL FEEL BETTER ABOUT YOURSELF!

Or maybe I need a sponsor like Nike "JUST DO IT! VOTE FOR ME!"

Will this help cast your vote: You *will* never pay taxes again.
I promise, I'll refund all your money. (P.C. P.C.
P.C.) You'll have free day care (even
if this means the U. S. will become a social state).
Socialism. I'll work gratis. Free
medical coverage for everyone. Would you vote for me
if I said no one has to work? You can stay home all day
watching *Love Connection*, because all we really want
is to be loved. You want
to be loved. I want to be loved
and I want to be President someday. Excuse me. I forgot
to mention my ultimate goal – to be your President. Yes,
I want to run the country. Vote for me
and you will be loved. I promise. *I will love you*
in my heart of hearts
dear voters for ever and ever and ever. (p.c.)

I'm a gentleman. I try projecting this image,
this quality to the world. It wasn't like I said to the girl
standing in the bank line, "God bless you! I hope
you're not coming down with a cold. And if

not, would you like to
take a ride in my new car? Have you ever
screwed on leather seats?" (n.p.c.) I didn't say anything
like that. It would have been rude
among the clientele, but what if I had
professed quite sincerely, "Bless you"
especially if no one sneezed? Would that make me
a heretic? Would I be
showing favoritism? I'd have to say, "Bless you"
to the man behind me, to the woman
on my side, to the tellers,
the branch manager. I'd have to stand
on the street corner handing out "Bless Yous"
to truckers on their way to deliver buns to McDonald's
or tires and polyester shirts to Wal-Mart. What about
                    the beautiful moms
with their cars loaded down with groceries
and melting *Sherbet*?

Am I being uppity? I apologize, if I am.
I am the common guy, like you, old Joe the barber.
The truckers – I know these guys would kick the crap out of me
if I said to them, "Bless you."
They'd call me a faggot.
Would it be politically correct
to defend myself or should I take it
like a man? (n.p.c.) Should I deny
my sexual lifestyle (n.p.c.) when they call
me a "queer" while kicking me in the head
with cowboy boots? (n.p.c.)

What? Leather seats in my car? (n.p.c.) Hey,
that was a several stanzas back. Let us move forward
with this thing, n'est-ce pas?
I didn't order leather seats.
They were standard. (n.p.c.) It's a fact

of my life – I don't wear furs, and I
loathe those who do. (p.c.) But leather
is from cows and cows are stupid
as dirt (n.p.c.) and we eat cows
because they can't outrun a sledgehammer, (n.p.c.)
and cows stand under the nearest tree
during a lightning storm. Stupid,
stupid, stupid! Yes, I'm sorry
(my head is hanging down in disgrace).
I have double grade (AA) egg on my face. I apologize.
I sincerely do. Cows have rights. (p.c.) Embryonic eggs,
chicken or otherwise, have rights, (p.c.) but listen up,
                    this is important: don't you have rights
to do with your body
as you choose? And isn't your body
your temple, and why
should I,
your President-to-be-elected, tell you
how to govern your body. It's your body;
not mine. (p.c.) And if you want to use
your body to have sex with me,
should I be allowed to stop you?   I think not!

If you will have sex with me
I'll have the seats
of my car replaced with a natural fabric. (p.c.)
Will cotton do?

Hey, I'm a looker, I admit. I look at anything
and, yes, you, reader of this poem, my comrades
with beautiful eyes and straight-white teeth, I gazed
(stared) at the young nimble girl (n.p.c.) standing in line
for at least a minute or two. I'm not big
on breasts, but I love a nice ass
and her ass was sweet-looking (n.p.c.)
                    like a peach

in a summer storm. Is it okay to say this
in our political atmosphere? Ass. (n.p.c.) Should I
even say I like women? (n.p.c.) Will this upset some men?
Will this upset those who are not sure
which sex they want to be? Will this
upset those few born with both sexes
that I haven't included them
in my pointed desire? I guess
I should just masturbate
while thinking of farm animals,
but then someone would accuse me of favoritism
if I thought too long on a particular animal.
Will it suffice to say that one of my fantasies
involves my lesbian friend? (p.c./n.p.c?) Pretty tame
stuff in comparison with your life; however,

I need to know: does this exclude
                    my homosexual male friends?
Who does this offend? Please, I implore you, write to me
in care of whatever magazine publishes this poem.
            I want to know
who you are so I can right a wrong. I'm flexible.
I want to be loved by everyone. Of course, I said it.
            I do like a nice ass. (n.p.c.)
I didn't say whether or not it was on a man
or a woman, (p.c.) but I'll say it now, set the record
straight, and I hope
I don't upset the other half of the world,
but as someone great must have once said, "Life is tough."
                    Yes, I like women,
and I like a pretty face, a sense
of humor, a strong intellect, a quick wit, and
a nice ass. And an intelligent woman
is an aphrodisiac. Maybe
ass is too crass, but rear
or rear end is what my mother says

and buttocks is too medical, so maybe it's just butt
which is a good word though maybe a bit bland, whereas ass
is a little steamy, a juicy word
that invokes sweat, and sweat invokes salt
and salt on a person's neck or shoulders
or ass is an aphrodisiac, too. And I get off on that. (N.P.C.)
I apologize. I'm just a man. Ass
certainly has atmosphere, and atmosphere is a word I like
sort of the way I like thought of falling
five thousand feet from an airplane, just spinning
and breathing cool air
as I rush toward our blue marble. Atmosphere
and ass are words that seem to surround you
like a good session with a (beautiful [n.p.c.]) woman
where all we do is lay together quietly (n.p.c.)
on the sofa with the lights low (n.p.c.)
listening to Natalie Cole's (p.c.) latest album
weave its way around the furniture like dry ice. We cuddle
and feel one another... (I know you,
you perverted dolt, you're thinking
I'll say we feel one another up [n.p.c.]),
                    but I'm not...
we feel one another breathing. Sometimes
I breathe in unison
with her. Yes! I like to cuddle (p.c.)
(such a babyish word). But I do.
So call me weak, call me sensitive. I admit it,
I like to cuddle, and now
all my men friends (n.p.c.)
in their macho, (n.p.c.) studly (n.p.c.) 4x4
wheel trucks (n.p.c.)
with gun racks (n.p.c.) loaded up for war, if they read
this, they'll poke fun at me.
But I do. I love to cuddle.
You can bet your ass
they'll say, "What do you mean

cuddling and no sex... why?" It's like what I read
years ago in *Playboy*: (N.P.C.) *The reason so many women*
fake orgasm is that so many men
fake foreplay. I don't understand
                    and please help me figure this out
if you can... why is there no Martin Luther King Drive
on the *Monopoly* board. What about housing
for the homeless, and do the B&O railroad
employees have a union? If you go to jail
is the Miranda Rule still viable? These are questions
that must be answered. Does *Trivial Pursuit* discriminate
against the uneducated? (p.c./n.p.c.?) Perhaps,
we need a witless version
with philosophical questions like "Why?"
with "Why not?" being the only acceptable reply.
How about a geographical question, "Name a city."

The other day at the grocery store
after having been to the bank
there was a person standing
in the vegetable section near
some onions. I noticed
that this person looked at me then
sneezed. I pushed my cart up the aisle
away from where this person was standing.

I could see this person needed a tissue
and the look on this person's
face said he/she would have liked
to have said *hello* to me, seen a smile, maybe a wink.
But I did not say a word. I kept on shopping
without saying one word and I pushed
my shopping cart, the one with four perfectly rotating wheels.

Old Timer

We knew the risk. Someone might get killed
as we hunted the enemy

in a cow pasture. We spied on old man Daniels,
a WWII munitions guy, still dazed

from Italy. With our Crossmen bb guns
we waged war, shooting his horse

in the flank and watched as he bucked wildly
like he'd rubbed against the electric fence.

One winter day, when the brush was gone
and snow drifts were all we could hide behind

we dinged his windows and laughed
until we heard the thick thud

pump from behind the barn
and then one hundred yards behind us, real mortar fire

and the ground exploding like a volcano. Four, five,
six rounds. As we ran across the open field

toward home a mile away, the strafe of live fire overhead
dropped us to the ground. The old bastard pinned us down

face flat for three hours in the snow. Then as we crawled
on our bellies like rats, he popped the snow in front

of us with silence, a sniper with a scope. One by one
he picked off the black birds overhead

on the telephone wire. Feathers and guts
fell on us. We stood out

like cockroaches in a bowl of rice in our blue coats
and didn't move for hours. Just when we thought

it was over, another bird exploded.
Then he was upon us, standing with his cloth strips

wrapped around his rifle, discolored from the war. He smelled
like boiled cabbage. "You boys had enough?"

We could barely answer. "Get on home
and get some dry clothes on." And as we ran,

he yelled, "Don't come back
until you can play for real." Then he laughed

like he was having fun and cupped
his hands around his face to light a cigarette.

Once in a Field
I Found a Place

where summers are gorgeous and grassy-full.
A field opens up like a catcher's mitt. Climb down
the hill, up the steep peak, where, out of breath,
puffing with blood pulsating, your body rushes,
relaxes like after making love. Take a deep
breath. Heart pump. There's a passage way
on top of the hill between moss clad walls
with bog-like flooring. Squeeze through.
Feel the water worm over your shoe lips.
Blue tulips! Unfold your body
into an open-air cavern. Eighty foot walls.
Smell the time-held dampness creep into your toad-skin.
Here you will find a golf ball-size hole
surrounded by dark moss
to your left by the slanted granite sheets. Climb
into the brunette grotto. It's a small hole.
Immediately you'll know something great is here.
In the hole you'll be alone, and listening,
and breathing slowly in a place
where light reflects darkness and pleasures
of madness are known only to madmen. If the telephone rings
the century changes. It's where intoxicated words whisper
the stalagmite's sweet secret drip of blue
and swirls the ocean's helix patterns into life.
Incredible things hide in here. It's as dark as coal
inside an apple. Apples bleed meaty white
when you eat them. You will discover a million apples
in this cave. Eat them all. Let their drip
drip from your chin. Let your electric mind race

back and forth until you feel absolute
silence or a wake of air brushing across your face
like a hand whooshing across water drawn for a bath.
Alone is something you'll miss when you leave. Here,
you can breathe and think, and everything is real
and great and unknown.

The Fraud Investigator Has a Vision Late One Afternoon

Looking out my bedroom window, I imagine
hanging down from the sky gigantic Plexiglas tubes,
between two and ten feet in diameter,
glaring like mirrors, illuminated
tubal timpani with ideas, great
ideas bouncing end to end like sound waves
and if you are listening, watching, observant,
the ideas will be yours.

I'm alert as a dog as I watch a cat
chase a squirrel through the snow and up a tree,
and a tall man jumps off the trolley car
of garbage. He hoists the can over
his shoulder and a log crackles
against my vision.

There are some things in life only I know
to be true – that everything travels to you
on parallel planes and axis. No instrument can measure
its delicate existence, but it's there
and has nothing to do with luck, and if your mind is open
to anything at a precise moment, it is yours.

Does my garbage man see the tubes
hanging from the sky? As the shorter man
pulled the compaction lever, he glanced up to my window.
I leaned behind the curtain.
What did I fear from him? Would he see
that I have no sympathy
for the world, that there is no death

more useful than that of someone else's.
He probably does not care, cold
and hungry, the stench of work
blistering his nose, and I'm sure he's thinking
of Charlotte Edwards' big tits in a sweat suit
running down the street, because I'm still
thinking of her ten minutes later. I can only imagine
the smell of the rotting waste
of other people's lives, and bet
that's how they judge a day's work.
Why am I thinking of tubes
hanging from the sky instead of the right words
placed side by side together
that would have Charlotte's shapely breasts in my hands?
What would I say? "Hello, Miss Edwards,
do you see the giant tubes
hanging from the sky?"

As the garbage men rode off, holding on
with one hand, the short guy threw a snowball
and missed. When the truck turned
the corner my garbage man bent down,
perhaps looking out
from under his Mets cap
to see the tubes (just one, maybe
for a brief instance) hanging in the sky
and he would think that maybe
there is something more. And,
if he does see the tubes will he be changed?
Straightening up, standing, he had in his hand
a half-eaten grapefruit,
and he threw it at the short guy
and hit him smack in the face.

The Tennis Player Goes Fishing with His Father

Darkness, darkness, forever black.
A child died today. We were new
to the lake, our summer alive

with freedom, our bodies
marshmallow white, eager
to ride the tire swing

like a bell rope clanging, swinging out
into the shy drip of our blue
voices screeching, R.E.M. singing

"Life, it's bigger, it's bigger than you
and you are not me" as if they knew
some great secret about you and me

and what we were driving towards
with the top down. Here the ambulance
tracks sliced into the muck

of the shore, a yawning mouth with slate
rock on the bottom claiming its kingdom
as I looked out over the calm forever.

Two boys no older than ten stood around
with mud in between their toes. The chubby one said,
"She looked like a tadpole."

I stood in silence by the oak, the dead
swing of the tire, time removed
like the square cut-out moments of our lives

we fold up and carry with us
into the thinness of the afternoon,
then into the night. The boys

whose job it was today to tell everyone
what happened, stood in expectation
as though I could walk that ashen girl

through her swimming lessons.
I realize now she was a dream waiting
for the world to wake up around her. Shadow

was the color she swam towards,
her arms stretching north
by northwest to the constellations

of her father's own bewilderment
and falling towards a single light.
If the world were different,

I'd be different. I'd bait penumbra
away from itself, away
from every fin-less child, towards the white

blinding our eyes. Darkness.
Darkness.
Forever black.

The Optical Illusion of Misinformation

My neighbor, Matt, stood at the front door
with a dead rabbit. The couple next to him

are on vacation but due home early.
He collected their mail

and newspapers. "What are you doing
with a dead rabbit?" I asked.

A gesture of goodwill, but I don't eat meat,
no smokes or drink, besides the rabbit was domestic

and covered with mud and blood. Matt had a worried crease
across his face, and around the corner

of the house, his Labrador, Buster,
sniffed and snorted the ground, sat

on the cool sidewalk staring at his white prize.
We washed away the blood and dirt

with warm water, *Ivory* soap,
and blow-dried the softness back in

as I do with my little girls after a bath.
The thought of buying a new rabbit

for the Reynold's occurred to us, but nothing
would be open on Sunday, not before

they returned, so like two thieves
returning stolen money to a bank vault,

we placed the rabbit in the wire cage
in their backyard, turned the rabbit upward on his side

to stare at the blue sky. Always a little squeamish,
Matt calls *Orkin* if bees swarm around his house

twice in one day. He was sick
to think he could forget

to feed and water the rabbit, then to have Buster
shake him until his neck snapped.

An hour after John and Lisa came home, as Matt
drew his arm across the table

to play the three of hearts
on the four of clubs, screams rang out

like a chainsaw ripping into an aluminum shed. Half
the neighborhood ran to their backyard

to stare at the clean white rabbit.
Lisa and John swore the rabbit died last week

and was buried under three small pine trees.
"Not anymore," I said. Everyone looked oddly

at me. Matt stood in the background like a dead tree
waiting to fall over. "Harv," I said,

"didn't you mow their yard yesterday?" I'm a lying
s.o.b., but we had heard Harvey's stories,

practical jokes, and years ago how he poisoned
his neighbor's hog because they slashed his new tractor tires.

What was I supposed to do – stand by
and let Harvey go free

for his years of lying? After that
everyone suspected him of everything

that happened in the neighborhood. Matt chained Blackie
to the porch and I dug a new grave

deeper and with as much emotion
as if burying a fifteen-year hunting dog.

We lugged a huge rock on top of it,
and eight months passed

before the Reynolds spoke to Harvey.
He kept to his side of the fence, and occasionally

I'd see him pounding a stake
to secure a sapling or practicing

his fly casting, trying to hit yellow rings
scattered throughout his backyard.

The Van Doris Paintings

I could feel your fugitive heart
        beating into me, a rapturous thump
of time, your presence

moving behind me in the dark
        closet as I hid from my daughters
in a game of hide and seek. The closet

was filled with canvases
        years forgotten, your portrait,
a frontal of furious colors

ripening like an apple in time-elapsed motion,
        beginning with your platinum hair
sifting through my fingers. When I asked what

you wanted for Christmas, you always said,
        "Just give me deep-forest green."
Night light burning, glowing

white against my daughters tucked in bed
        like gifts in a stocking, I spread
the paintings against the wall, naked

cards from a stag deck. You stared
        back with the tequila smile that led me
years ago to wander away from my ordinary life, entangled

in your silk, your uselessness for college
        and your legs spread
like the distance between night and day. I'd forgotten

about the gold frame we bought
　　　　at Bob's Junk Shop, a rainy Sunday
of marbles splattering against the car

roof as we wrestled
　　　　to get at one another
on a dirt road near Athens. Still,

I see the mark, the spark I captured
　　　　in your eyes when my world was a canvas
of pomegranate appetites in a rusted out Honda

driving you back, back further home.
　　　　I thought I could be a lover of colors
and time when what I was searching for

was truth, but truth is a homeless beauty
　　　　asking for a night of comfort
who sometimes marries into the family.

Maybe truth is just the absence
　　　　of nothing to lie about. Your eyes
quenched my uncertainties while you searched

through me like a thief ransacking a dresser drawer.
　　　　I have continued to search for truth
in the chunks of clay I cut from the river bed

at my sister's farm, hauling
　　　　the load to the barn with the *John Deere* tractor,
covering the trailer under a damp tarp.

I never worry about you returning
　　　　with our story, when my life was unrealized.
After this long everything finds its own truth

and turns to love. What we think is right
           is sometimes only right
for that moment, then evaporates

into gossamer, colors changing
           into a world so completely new
and moving forward in spectacular clarity.

III
Double-Live Cowboy

I've been everywhere, man
I've been everywhere, man
Crossed the deserts bare, man
I've breathed the mountain air, man
Travel - I've had my share, man
I've been everywhere

– Johnny Cash

and then I felt much better
but not
entirely
so

– Charles Bukowski

As Sunday Morning Was Coming Down

-for David Bottoms

On a dirt road deep in south Georgia, a dark stick stretched
across the dust, belly full of rat
or small rabbit, eons of meanness
sensing the vibrations as my truck slowly rolled
to a stop near the dark rattler.

His tongue flickered softly
as he tasted the air
for my leg. I stood transfixed, listening
to the Nashville sounds of Chet Atkins' guitar,
staring from twenty feet, not really
far enough away, but close enough
to spring to the hood if he suddenly moved.

His body swelled flat against the road to show his girth
and intemperance as he flickered motionless. I backed away,
heart pounding. I returned to the truck
and watched for any movement. Minutes passed,
then finally, video camera poised in my hand, I stepped closer,
fifteen feet perhaps, maybe
less, kicked a foot load of gravel
toward the ancient lizard. Curled up and postured,
I wondered how far can he really strike?

What love he had was only for passing
across the road to the sun-warmed rocks
to sleep another day and pay back
the debt of his old life. As I filmed, I waited

and waited for the black smile of his mouth to open
wide for the camera, to see deep
into the darkness of his body.

Puffed violence of antiquity,
it was hard to believe
that anything
so perfectly still
could ever move again.

A Woman Taking Off
Her Shoes

I rested my elbows on the hard wood bar, pale blue
neon lights flashed between the ceiling fan and the crack

of pool balls. I watched through the barroom mirror
at the woman who was silky as the velvet night

along the Platte River in winter, where men go camping
and listen to their worn stories as they stare off into the loneliness

of infinity, dreaming of a woman like this and how she must go
armed or go beautiful. Beneath the bar stool

her legs rubbed together as she spoke to a short bearded man
sipping brandy and nodding his rooster head to the $100 bet.

Her heels popped out of her shoes
as she wiggled her feet in and out, which made me think

she wasn't taking them off for any guy
this evening. Swishing the backwash of *New Castle*

in my mouth, I remembered the voice of an old friend, years ago,
called out in a lawn game. Her eyes, closed, like that summer's diary

in a Chevy truck, our bodies fastened to the darkness
in a sticky Mississippi corn field

and her shirt split open like a cotton boll
as I lifted off her cranberry smile, tasting

the smell of her hair. Suddenly
the woman caught me staring, a two-ball

bank-shot combination to a corner pocket where the deep blue haze
of remembrance filled the room. She fiddled with her shooter, twisted

the straw to her tongue. She had sized up the room and knew
I wasn't gambling. I nodded to the bartender for a hit of *Comfort*,

then noticed the combinations of her legs, her feet rubbing
together, scratching her nylons like a sweet summer song.

Things I Should
Be in Jail For

Speeding! Not just speeding
a few miles over the limit, but 110 m.p.h.
straight through from Augusta to Atlanta

in my sporty little car. Or 140 m.p.h.
in the Vermont countryside on a cloudy morning,
the tires bounding off the ground then sliding

from pavement to gravel. I survived
the 90 m.p.h. spin out. I'm not reckless,
it's just that I like to open it up

once in a while. Women, more than a few
should have had me locked up for handing out heartbreak
like one-liners. I've had my face slapped

a few times for popping the wrong question. Everyone thinks
they know prank phone calls, "Do you have Prince Albert in a can?"
"Is your refrigerator running?" Ha! Ha!

Better let him out; better catch it before it runs away.
Try calling a total stranger and convincing him
the Fed Ex truck is broken down ten miles away. Can you

pick up the package on Canton Highway in the K-Mart parking lot?
I've done some pretty crummy things
in my life, but still, I pay my taxes, every single penny,

every year, not because I like to
but who wants the I.R.S. poking you in the eye? And I don't cheat
at golf. I play the ball were it lies. Practical jokes, how about

an intervention for a friend who doesn't drink, then his parents
getting angry at his insistent denial. I have
an ongoing feud with my garbage man

because he complained of too much trash. "Just wait,"
I thought. I've disguised it all – car batteries
and bags of cement wrapped up like dead fish.

A month of newspapers in quadrupled Hefty bags,
then fifty gallons of water to sweeten the deal. "Lift that!"
Shovel fulls of dirt. Just dirt. Real heavy dirt. And

if I could add extra gravity to it, I would. It's not like I'm Rambo
starting a war, but one day, I had some extra garbage to unload
and he jumps on me for it. Did I mentioned Atlanta to Boston

(1400 miles) in sixteen hours? That's *Indianapolis 500* fast!
In my home town, no one locks their doors
when going to church. I've walked through their houses,

not touching anything, just looking, deeply smelling the fried bacon
and coffee still lingering in the air. Then I leave. Week after week
they go to church. Then there is the dream

of the dead body, a reoccurring nightmare
like a girl you slept with a couple of times
and she keeps calling and calling, wanting to know when

you're getting together again and if you really
love her. She just keeps calling
from across town in her small upstairs studio apartment

with the noisy toilet, blue and yellow butterfly wallpaper, and a cat
named Cooper. I've made and sold moonshine. I've tossed a few
dead fish in my neighbor's car engine before he heads out

on vacation. I've never done drugs, but
I've sped through a huge mud puddle
and splashed a man standing at the bus stop

all decked out in a suit and tie. Of course, that isn't
against the law, just demonstrates my general disregard
for, well, pretty much everything. I've stolen

enough office supplies to restock IBM and I've swiped
two newspapers at a time for years. But it's the dream
of the dead body that keeps following me from town to town,

house to house, buried in the basement
or backyard, somewhere where my eyes give me away
to the police. It's just a dream and I know it

is all the stuff I've ever gotten away with rolled up
into a Sisyphus-type boulder just bounding
down the hill, a rolling thunder

life sentence chiseled with my name. I feel a little twinkle
of naughtiness in my smile as I mature and figure I'll end up
like Jack Lemmon in *Grumpy Old Men* – innocently

breaking the law in a rather sweet way that endears me
to scores of women wanting an older man who isn't afraid
to tell some kid in a Mustang to shove it

straight up his ass as I rip past him, angry
because old age and loneliness are so close
around the corner, coupled with my regret for not stealing more kisses.

Three Short Poems

Il Escaplo

I have fought too often
      with words, and now war
is the color of my lover's eyes.

Migratory Animals

Currents running under the crystal
      road - four men, snow mobiles
plunge through the lake like penguins.

Suspicions

Look at the person next to you
      and imagine the worst thing
they could do in their life.

Creating the Illusion of Intrigue

A local newspaper took an interest
in me so when the girl called

for an interview, I agreed, but told
her to bring

a case of *Sam Adams Lager*. She didn't
know I rarely drink. I wanted to see

how serious she was, so
when she arrived, I expected her

to be about twenty, but
she had more wrinkles

than an elephant's ass. But
she did bring the beer.

My wife told her
that we were

having a Super
Bowl party next weekend and

she was welcome
to bring a friend. I thought,

"A young intern would be nice." I did
the interview and was witty

and charming, as
always, but I would not

comment any further on my
five-year stint in prison for

robbing a bank. I can't
figure out where she got such a story

in the first place or who
might have suggested the idea.

Jonathan

My friend's mother died
when we were eight
and not knowing
what death was
or what to do, we sat
in her closet
and played
Connect the Dots
until his father came home
from the hospital.

As we quietly played
I could smell her
standing next to us.

It's difficult, if not impossible,
at eight, to understand
the impact of a mother's death
until years later
when you are an adult
and can travel
to those secret places
where we hide
from the world.

Within a few months
my family moved
to Texas and my friend stayed behind
and lived his entire life
in the same small town.

The Skip Trace

My mother and father asked me to locate some old friends
from high school. I began the slow search

by packing the car and returning home,
reliving my childhood in towns

scattered across the country. I walked the streets
and dirt roads to my old houses to see who is living there now,

took a few photographs, stopped by the old school, the baseball lot
and my grandfather's old house. At K-Mart, I ran into a woman I knew

when she was a young girl. I kissed her
once at a birthday party behind the staircase

in the basement. Now, she has grown children
who quite possibly are more mature

than I will ever be, but this time, I manage
to leave town without getting tossed in jail. One by one

I found my parents' friends. I searched
and searched for anyone they could call, to reminisce,

because I did not want to return empty-handed.
I made the slow visit home

and over a cup of coffee, I told my parents
that everyone they once knew had died.

I showed them the photographs
of our old houses and the snow buried very deeply.

I did not tell my parents I kissed that woman
many years ago behind the staircase

in the basement when the lights were low.
And she kissed me back with her eyes closed.

Thoughts on Sighting a UFO: Montpelier, Vermont

I have swum with humpbacks off the California coast
and I have seen grizzly bears
in Alaska sitting in a grassy field stretching
their necks, following geese across the plum sky
like fish too quick to catch.

In the silent street
we leaned against the car, pressed our
minds farther out to astral desires, wondered
if the lights we saw stretching time
and time again across the black glass
of sky in episodic heart beats were illuminating
for us. We could have been swept away
by a tornado in the darkness as we searched
for a greater light. Everything is
a metaphor for love. The air
can be brisk, yet warm. You were
beauty leaning against the breath
of the blackberry evening, and everywhere you walked
the scent of scandal lingered.

Even in your pulchritudinous earthsuit I wanted you
to see what I could hardly understand,
how looking into the farthest depths
of someone close to us, love can be
distant, yet still within sight.

The Tyburn Tree

Yellow prairie dirt
dried like sun-baked marrow
from the bones of stranded cattle
swirls across the plains
as sagebrush tumbles
past the edge of town. Horses scuffle,
branches from the tyburn tree slap
in rhythm to the wind, whispers
pass among the townsfolk.
The preacher wipes his neck
with a sweat-stained handkerchief
and a card player dude spits
tobacco juice and complains
about the dealer last night.
The crack of a hickory switch
sends the black mare chasing
the muddy banks of a watering hole
and a man with his hands tied
behind his back twists
from the tyburn tree.

Posting Bail

Love's boozy moon follows me
everywhere, drunk, jail time slapping

me in the face as the cuffs are squeezed
around my wrists for yelling her name

at two in the morning. My friend, Matt, who bailed me out,
told me on the wet drive home as ice streaked

off the windshield like threads of light, if I am ever stuck
in a boat on the ocean with a hooker, the one thing

I don't need at sea is the fear
of going down. His laughter broke the silence

of self-pity for this double-live cowboy
who rides the lawnmower like he's taming the West.

Everyone was home today for Christmas dinner
when I returned to stare out the quiet kitchen window

at the birds in the yard making a living. This is where
we find ourselves, our ordinary lives waiting

for the world to dry up in disillusionment. There is a shadow
within my shadow and that shadow-guy is the culprit, the bad guy

inside me doing all these things. He's like a compass
directed straight toward trouble. I've searched for self-discovery

bar hopping (I almost wrote "bra hopping" which is also true).
Just marry me off to someone who will put up with everything.

If every once in a while the bears, panthers, and wolverines
ate mankind out of existence that would be fine with me.

Directions Home

Four a.m., the bars down
past their last drip
of syrup, the shy slip
of evening nursing its last hunger.
Stopped at a traffic light,
I see the signs' slight
drag of morning, the slow nothing
of drowsed houses
pulling me, carousing
against my groin, tempting like a whore
rolling her garter
beyond mid thigh. I barter
for the evening, for my life
to reach an accord
with my mislaid vows, the illuminated hoard
of messages I've missed. Is this where I should be? The signs
do not answer. I give them time
but instead the ghost traffic piles up deeper at the intersection
like a game of *Buck Buck* in meditation.

In Heaven, all dogs howl as much as they like. When I'm gone
I won't be gone, I will howl everlasting.
Soon I'll sleep, dream about the sign's
brief messages to me: "The blind
see only darkness, know only light – Repent now!; Help
the economy – going out of business sale; Dine
here!" Now I'll pursue the straight lines
running white, but five years ago I would have laid rubber
on this street, opened an aperture
to the world, sounding my arrival or my departure.

Germination

I remember when you soaked corn seeds in a coffee can
and I walked with you through the till of the garden
down the narrow rows of cabbage and zucchini

and you reached down for a fist of soil,
squeezed the minerals tight into a ball
then broke it up. You rolled a handful

of seeds between your fingers,
catching one beneath your thumb
and dropping it like a lure

precisely where you aimed.
With the side of your boot you pushed
the seed into darkness.

There is a new family living in your house
and after forty-five years your garden
is gone. The tires crunching on the gravel

driveway are gone, too, and you
no longer stand on the back porch
waving good-bye. But sitting down the street in my car, I think

how nice the house looks painted light green
and maybe they still play croquet in the backyard.
They should have never uprooted your blueberry bushes.

So maybe, one quiet night in late November
when they are in Florida for the holidays
I will return and burn their house to the ground.

Hunting with Chuck

I once shot a man with a 9mm
I told my friend as we sat in the tree
stand because I wanted him to know
that I could kill something. I didn't
want him to think I was a sissy, so I accepted
his invitation to bring home dinner
for the entire year.

So when the doe spread her legs
and sniffed for what the air
would not give her, she drank, and
as Chuck brought the rifle to his steady breath,
I said *let this one go*. And the next
and the next, until he realized
that I was a perfectionist and wanted
a ten point buck. But what I really wanted
was to show him that I could shoot
a man and watch him bleed
and not have to bring it home with me.

Thirty Minutes Before Sundown

It meant to me
that beauty and terror were intertwined so powerfully
and went so deep that any kind of love
can fail.

      – Robert Hass

If only I could nudge you from this sleep
My maimed darling, my skittery pigeon.
Over this damp grave I speak the words of my love:
I, with no rights in this matter,
Neither father nor lover.

      – Theodore Roethke

Turning Towards White

I am a virgin again. I cleared my throat
against this dark cave

of marriage, now I am pure
again, like a young woman whose heart beats

to have a finger slide down between the elastic
of her underwear, to the halved peach, dreaming

of the breathlessness of a tongue
stealing her words, turning her saliva into champagne.

I can still feel your heart
beating a million miles away

and wonder which of us will love first,
again, love a stranger, the substitution

for what we are denying in one another
until we are just shadows of our familiar.

I have killed you many times
with my words and lived on

until you killed me
with your ruthless shock

that knocked me into the conscience
of my other being. Last night,

as the days switched over
I blew out my candles again,

over and over, wish after wish
until the Gods were tired

enough to make it happen. The words
no longer are important,

their meanings,
but poems are all I have

to give, not nearly
enough to bring back

the breathlessness of our world.
I saved the candles, and now realize

why you saved everything
about me in your cardboard box.

Marriage

Walking in the woods you find a matchbox.
Crawl into it.
Avoid standing in one place, jump
from black and white linoleum
squares to a teddy bear baptism
and back. Feel the seams
with your palm-flats.
There is nothing
like a death sentence
to clear the mind. Fly
from your intellect, swing
beneath the leaves, retrieve
yourself by breathing ether
waves of light. We never escape
the strangeness of beauty. Step out
of the box. Leap into my arms.

Room 428 at the Days Inn Hotel: Montpelier, Vermont

There is nothing outside to remind me that this is America,
except the GULF sign revolving like a huge wafer
of butter. Today, I can be anyone

from anywhere as I stare out the window
catching the crisp sun, the afternoon view
of a street café, movie theatre, and a beautiful woman,

my friend, Alexandra, is reading my poems,
laughing. At the writing table
I sit, palms holding my chin as if my hands

cupped together could steady her in my naked mind,
like little postcards spread out, each an individual bed
of beautiful scenery I could dive into

like a heated swimming pool.
Though I could be anywhere
in the world, the radio station

tells me it's the outskirts of Paris, swaying
red sounds, (is this love?) the attached feeling
of something new, like when the sky opens up

after a week of rain, refreshed, cleansed
with a sense of infinite possibilities. But what is love
except lust's naive sister? What is lust

but the craziness of... well, who knows. Yet,
it's here beside me. I'm questioning everything,
trying to find a truth. I am a man

who watches the snow fall out of the empty sky
and wonders what would happen if I no longer believed
in the wheel, would everything go flat,

would clocks stop running?
A corner room with a queen-size bed,
the shower pressure dribbles. The heater

warms the room quickly, but we stay layered
in sweaters as commitment to our lives.
Next door the wall grunts of love making,

a famous writer I admire, but I try to ignore
the headboard thumping. Thumping, beating
like my anticipation when she reads my secret thoughts,

and how dinner and a long slow walk
up snowy steps can surrender us
into our arms' disguise, rescue

the ordinary life. Laughter
is my only crevice into a woman's heart,
and as Alex laughs, her lips slice

thinly when she looks up
at me. How deeply,
and is this enough, I wonder. O, God

of all the Gods there have ever been
or will be on this infatuated earth,
I would love to touch her

lips with mine, press her into me, but
we are married to different feelings
and I know the hotel would collapse

in fever. I want to absorb her
into my porous heart, run away
to Greece and live

in the bleached houses, read
everything in translation. I want to drink
the pomegranate juices dripping off her breasts, rub

these juices into her skin, deep
swirls of red, lift her arching back
and swallow the juices caught in her navel.

The Ordinary Life of a Sculptor

Walk through the front door of my house
anytime the lights are on and listen

to the wind brush against the shingles
or the neighborhood children

in pyramids reaching for avocados
in my back yard. Down the hall,

third door on the right, there is a woman
standing on a table, clay molded

from memory of all the perfect bodies
I have held. In adoration

I have loved a thousand women
from a distance, a particular motion of balance

as they opened a car door or circled
their hand in a purse looking

for a certain item, then snapping the clasp
as though the world were safe.

Last month standing in the ticket line,
a pair of hands, eyes

(I call them orbs, blue
orbs, chestnut orbs, starburst orbs) staring

so matter-of-factly at the movie posters.
It was the curve of this woman's neck

from her ears to shoulders I remember,
one smooth line. I press my thumbs

against the clay pulse, breathe
in and bring life to this sculpture.

It is not easy to sculpt only flesh,
each piece is internal, attitude,

form, like the summer squalls
I watch through the wall of windows

roar low and hard over the ocean.
This sculpture is you, Muse,

the potpourri of all the beautiful women
in the world. You are every one of them combined

into a graceful spirit, but whose husband
left you to think about the years. Men

are bastards. I know and hope
this does not hurt, but no man

will leave without another woman waiting,
because I, too, have felt the need

to abandon the ordinary life. It hurts me
to see your lips tighten and the lump of pain

like a fist rolled in your stomach, so I try
to make you laugh, find a way into your heart,

but it is not me in all ways I try. But, still
I love you deeply and all your beauty

that sends men crying your name into the darkness
we call infatuation. When men walk the echoing halls

of an art gallery, they see you
in every color and shape of every painting

and sculpture, they see you in every corner
they turn, looking back upon themselves

because what they feel for you
is moving beautifully though their body.

Robert Walks His Dogs

Last night the phone rang at two o'clock.
I walked my dogs along the sleepy shore, pointed
to the Little Dipper. Roger looked at me

like it was a black day, Jack
grabbed Roger's collar, twisted him to the sand, off
they ran chasing the cool breeze of ghosts.

Through the open door of the rented condo, a young
boy yelled, called his mother an ugly bitch.
I wanted to be the boy's missing father, beat

the hell out of him. I needed to pound him
as badly as he needed a beating. Last week
I meet the boy's divorced mother as the waves'

lifting motion grimaced like faces
from years of shipwrecks and undertows.
She's not my type, but nice

enough, curlers spun tight, a scarf to cover
her coiffured art work. She needed help
planting the beach umbrella, offered me a beer.

The following day she showed up
at my wall of windows, tapped a *Coors* can
and smiled for my attention. The potter's wheel slowed.

Covered in clay – I had started a vase
several times – I asked her in. She inspected
each sculpture, vase, and relief while jabbering wildly

about the weather, her hometown in Ohio.
"I could model for you if you'd like.
I know you have naked sculptures,

but I wouldn't mind. Really."
I was working on the vase (however uninterested),
but said I would call her first

if this changed. She shouldn't have
worn a bikini I thought, a one piece (perhaps), solid color.
She'd look cute in a ponytail and jeans. She had a nice

laugh, but I could tell
that somewhere in life she'd turned left,
no longer knowing what made her beautiful.

When I caught up to Jack he had a horseshoe crab in his mouth.
The beach was covered with floating stones
moving between both worlds. I set him free.

I pointed Roger toward the stars again, "If you travel
through the Little Dipper you can go back in time,
through the Big Dipper you can see the future."

The condo door slammed and the air
between the anchored ship lights split
on the horizon. Jack and Roger,

still as marble statues, stared
at the boy spinning out, kicking sand, running away
until the dogs figured he was just another ghost

crying in the wind. I knew his mother
could no longer control him. Tomorrow I would
ask her to sit for me, clothed. She has a pain I need.

The Movie

This is Your Life – front row,
the most comfortable seat you've ever sat in, contouring
your body's every move. White room,
contemporary California marble stretches the walls,
box speakers, sound system of angels, audible hierarchy.

A door in the wall opens – an apparition
of old friends, relatives long dead walk the aisle
to shake your hand, say "Hello, Frank. How in Hell
have you been?" They came to see the film
of your life, cute layers
of birthday cake smeared across your face,
the first day of school, the neighbor's cat
buried to his neck in the backyard, the lawn mower
that wouldn't crank so you doused him with lighter fluid.

Nothing is spared. You cover your eyes.
Angels strap your arms. You close your eyes,
old angel surgeons remove your eyelids, cherub
nurses wipe their foreheads. Friends kick at your seat,
laugh and cheer at your slick moves
when you pick up a waitress in Palm Springs, a sawbuck
and a note to meet you at the Marriott
for drinks. Your wife, dead three years, listens
as you tell a whore in Omaha, "Jello moves
more than my wife when I eat it." Everyone laughs.
You were a funny guy.

To the side of the screen
under an arch, an angel scores
your performance, down 148-171, the good versus bad,
but you know you did more good, and for awhile
you hit straight marks

for each boy you taught to play football,
how they developed a sense of worth over the years.
At the end of the aisle two boys, killed
in the war, lean forward to thank you
for the time you spent, how much you meant to them.
Scenes of your kindness abound.

The film pans to life's hypothetical "what ifs".
The San Francisco job – you'd have been fired
within two months, loved the city
enough to become city planner. Whatever happened
after you glued the gas gauge full
on the beat-up blue Pontiac?
– the old man's wife ran out of gas
in Texas, the heat sucked out her heart.

An unlimited engagement:
You will weep, and each day
there's an hour break
when you'll be led to a friend's movie,
your wife's movie, Elvis' or Lincoln's movie.
You see, Frank, no one
is above reproach, but you won't laugh
at them, humiliated even for what they've done.
Shuffling back to your room, the usher hands you a broom.
Laughter from the movie down the hall echoes
as you sweep the popcorn puffs across the floor.

Under the breath and swell of warmth
rolled in your body, you wonder
if God has taken to you. Your mind is more clear
than when you spun in the tunnel of light
you fell through. It feels like only moments ago
you slammed on the brakes
to avoid a tractor-trailer jackknifed,
and if you hadn't been jack-legged
you might have seen the wall of jagged steel.

A Blind Date for Gilbert and Skeeter

When Gilbert O'Sullivan sings "Alone Again Naturally"
I want to cry. Every time
his voice stops me cold. I am vulnerable

and hopeless and my chest
feels like the silent shell
of a rusted-out car.

After twenty years there's an accord
with his life and mine. I don't know
if this poem is about Gilbert or me, but

why is it so painful
for Mr. O'Sullivan? And for me?
When he recorded "Alone Again Naturally" did he know

I would always feel as miserable
as when everything he touched disappeared?
I learned a lesson that maybe he wasn't trying to teach

and this is just the result: Never love
anything that can die.
But isn't this too abstract? Shouldn't it be

like Harry Chapin's lady blue
who ruined her gown and the unsalvageable future
of the taxi driver in the hard San Francisco rain,

or Janis Ian cheating at solitaire, each rejected card
a boy she had a crush on, covered up
and reshuffled. It's been five years now

since I last heard how Gilbert's mother died,
and I listen to the radio, whether in traffic
or late night in a steady rain

in a quiet southern town
sipping a cup of coffee with the lights off.
It's a game I play

to keep this Big Adventure interesting:
pick a song and wait to see
how long it takes to hear

that song on the radio.
So Gilbert (who is perhaps waiting
in Malibu, California in a Taco Bell for his loneliness

to creep away) must know
that we can never be certain
who is secretly in love

with us. Maybe Gilbert condemned himself
to eternal rejection
years ago when he recorded his song.

And it's the same when I hear Skeeter Davis
cry out in "End of the World."
I cry along with her because I remember

being dumped for another guy (many times).
Is Skeeter still in that kind of pain?
I've moved on to other arrows,

but no one entirely abandons
a Skeeter Davis kind of pain.
Perhaps Skeeter is like me, dreaming

of someone in her life, but waking up
with the sheets tangled.
What kind of guy destroys a spirit

like Skeeter's? She's the girl
so quintessential to America:
the beach, blonde hair, the All-American

high school sweetheart in a Beach Boys' song,
the girl every guys wants to be with.
Did Skeeter learn to stay away

from this kind of guy? I believe in revenge
– and if she didn't
here's my suggestion – put his picture

on an album cover, a wanted poster: STAY AWAY
FROM THIS HEART BREAKER! I Should
write to Gilbert and Skeeter,

tell them to stay away
from lovers like this. Think
of the love story, the paparazzi,

if I could talk them into meeting
me at Redondo Beach, the sun setting,
a small round table, two chairs, a bottle

of *Ferrari Cerano*. I'd leave them to talk.
Skeeter could forget that other guy
and Gilbert wouldn't be alone.

They could record an album, have a Christmas
special with Andy Williams, sing
and get married on prime-time Sunday night.

This all reminds me of a story
of a Belgian Sheep Dog, Fido,
[who] *trekked almost 1,000 miles across*

> *Europe in a two-year search for his former owners. The dog's*
> *odyssey began in 1989 after his owners, Jose and Lise, left him*
> *in a dog home in Belgium after moving to Spain. The kennel*
> *promised to find Fido a new owner. Jose and Lise thought*
> *they'd seen the last of Fido, [until] Lise stepped out of her house*
> *near the city of Gijon to go shopping and almost stumbled over*
> *Fido. Jose and Lise could not explain how Fido found them since*
> *he had never been to Spain. They plan to reward him for his*
> *epic journey by giving him a lifetime home.*

Not everything returns home,
so you can't be careless
with love. Unlike Fido, push hard enough

and everything goes away.
Gilbert O'Sullivan. Skeeter Davis.
Belgium Sheep Dogs... it's not the distance

but the intent of returning home
that counts, and home
is not distance but time, and when

the years creep along out of reach,
the impossibility of returning
to where deep waters flow

is like reaching out from the grave.
I'm not lonely as I follow my bliss
and listen to more than just sad songs,

but sad songs take me back
to a teenager too scared to say hello
to a girl. We all know this girl

so absolutely golden
and perfect that the world
would collapse inward

if there was the slightest chance that she
even knew your name. Call it innocence,
or shyness or romantic, but for a brief moment

Oliva Newton-John's daydreamy voice
singing "Hopelessly Devoted to You" connects
me to this golden girl, who by now

I am certain does not remember me. But I'm okay
with that. I've stopped holding on
and now I'm waiting to live

the mystery of my life,
to bring Gilbert and Skeeter together,
let them know the debt

from their old life is paid off
and happiness is easier than the stars
passing in front of the moon.

Happiness is obtainable. I probably
shouldn't tell you this, but I'd like
to ask Olivia Newton-John

out on a date. I'd pack up the car
with a picnic basket and CD player,
drive her to the beach at midnight.

At sunrise we would walk together, stop
to watch the pelicans
kiss the ocean's lips. For Gilbert

and Skeeter hopefully
love is just around the corner.
A beach. A table. A bottle

of wine, and the sky stretched out
and filled with enough stars
to equal each time they've cried

for someone, each time
they've fallen back
into the brevity of darkness

and pain moving between a stone mattress.
Maybe all they need is someone
to cup their hands together

in a world where we arrive in a sea of thrashing
mnemonics. Can it be this simple?
We can stop singing: Her kisses are the moon

away, her love is twice as far.
And although the world isn't quite the same
since Johnny Carson went off the air,

if Skeeter and Gilbert will meet me
at Redondo Beach thirty minutes before sundown
I can promise them something.

Bad Ticker

I can feel it, deep inside, a broken clock
that correctly tells time twice a day,

skipping unexpectedly, the swelling
of something wrong like the serpent in *Alien*

ready to explode outward. I lay in bed
and feel the thickness waxing

and there is so much I want
to say and do and I try to sleep but

fear overtakes my mind
because I cannot yet leave

with (so much) everything to teach
my children. So here I am,

an insomniac wandering the house
late at night and into the morning hours, tucking

my children under the bed covers, and my dog
not far from the grave wobbles with me, helping me

through this journey. The other day,
driving down Peachtree Road toward *Brusters,*

my four-year-old son told me that banana split
rhymes with sharing, and I wish I could help him

understand that they have made me a better man
than I could have ever hoped or dreamt to have been on my own.

Notes

Dr. I. Lamar Maffett, for whom the book is dedicated, was the first professor I had at Dekalb College, now Georgia Perimeter College, who took a genuine interest in my academic education and my interest in writing poetry. He gave me scores of encouragement during my few years there. He was an incredibly humorous man and a great influence on my life. He is the subject in the elegy, "The Letter Back Home."

The quote from Czeslaw Milosz is from the poem, "Return to Krakow in 1880."

The quote from James Dickey is from the poem, "Cherrylog Road."

"Chilean Nights": The term *duende* means "the power to attract through personal magnetism and charm."

"The Death that Never Occurred": Antom Sigular (1829-86) is my great-great-grandfather. He fought for the Union Army in the Civil War out of Chautauqua County, New York. My wife's family, out of South Carolina, fought for the Confederacy.

"Mowing the Yard of a Woman Whose Name I Have Forgotten": At the end of this poem when the mother covers up the child's footprints — this story was heavily borrowed from a 1988 conversation I had with the poet, A.R. Ammons.

The quote from Richard Hugo is from the poem, "Degrees of Gray in Philipsburg."

The quote from Robert Penn Warren is from the poem, "Three Darkenesses."

"Tuesday Morning in My Old Neighborhood": In the late 1960s or early 1970s, a house near where I lived in western Pennsylvania blew up as a result of a leaky gas line. No one was injured.

"Once in a Field I Found a Place": The cave-like area described in this poem is located behind the campus of Vermont College, specifically in the woods behind Noble Lounge.

"The Tennis Player Goes Fishing with His Father": The lyrical quote is from R.E.M. — "Losing My Religion."

The quote from Johnny Cash is from the song, "I've Been Everywhere."

The quote from Charles Bukowski is from the poem, "the famous writer."

"Il Escaplo": defined as "the one who got away."

"Directions Home": "Buck Buck" is a childhood game where one person bends over and holds on to a tree or telephone pole and the other children run and jump on his back until the "tree holder" can no longer hold on, thus falling to the ground.

The quote from Robert Hass is from the poem, "On Squaw Peak."

The quote from Theodore Roethke is from the poem, "Elegy for Jane."

"A Blind Date for Gilbert and Skeeter": the story of the Belgian Sheep Dog, Fido, is a true account taken from a newspaper article that showed up on the wire services.

The cover painting is *Irish County Lane* by the American artist, Eliesh O'Neil Lane, who resides in Tucker, Georgia. A special thanks to my parents for permission to reprint the painting.

Skeeter Davis, one of the subjects in "A Blind Date for Gilbert and Skeeter," died in Nashville, TN on September 20, 2004 at age 72. She was a member of the *Grand Ole Opry*. Her first hit was in 1953, *I Forgot More Than You'll Ever Know*, recorded with Betty Jack Davis as the Davis Sisters. Her other top ten hits included *Set Him Free* (1957), *(I Can't Help You) I'm Falling Too* (1960), *My Last Date (With You)* (1961), and her signature international hit *The End of the World* (1963). In 1985, she and the rock band NRBQ collaborated on a critically acclaimed album called *She Sings, They Play*. Her 1993 autobiography is called *Bus Fare From Kentucky*.

William Walsh was born in Jamestown, NY in 1961 and though he has lived throughout the United States, he has spent most of his life in the south. He resides in Atlanta with his wife and three children. His dog, Roger, (pictured here) recently passed away at age seventeen.

He primarily earns a living in unrelated fields, but on occasion lectures and instructs on creative writing. Over the years, he has taught English Literature, creative writing, and composition at La Grange College, Dekalb College, Oglethorpe University, the Atlanta College of Art, and the Chautauqua Institute. He received an A.B. from Georgia State University and an M.F.A. from Vermont College. For the past ten years he has worked as a private investigator.

He is the author of *Speak So I Shall Know Thee: Interviews with Southern Writers,* McFarland and *The Ordinary Life of a Sculptor* (a chapbook), Sandstone. He has also interviewed Noble Laureates Czeslaw Milosz and Joseph Brodsky, as well as such international writers as Ariel Dorfman. He has written for newspapers and magazines, and has served on the editorial board of several literary magazines. An avid golfer and tennis player, he has won numerous tournaments in each event, most recently the 2004 U.S.T.A. Georgia State Championship and the 2004 U.S.T.A. Southern Sectional Championship (both team tennis). This is his first collection of poems.